robin fulton

TREE-LINES

BOOKS BY ROBIN FULTON

POETRY

INSTANCES (Macdonald, Edinburgh, 1967)
INVENTORIES (Caithness Books, 1969)
THE SPACES BETWEEN THE STONES
    (New Rivers, 1971)
THE MAN WITH THE SURBAHAR
    (Macdonald, Edinburgh, 1971)
TREE-LINES (New Rivers, 1974)

TRANSLATIONS

FIVE SWEDISH POETS
    (Seton Hall University, 1972)
SELECTED POEMS OF LARS GUSTAFSSON
    (New Rivers, 1972)
SELECTED POEMS OF GUNNAR HARDING
    (London Magazine Editions, 1973)
SELECTED POEMS OF TRANS TRANSTROMER
    (Penguin Books, 1974)
SELECTED POEMS OF OSTEN SJOSTRAND
    (Oleander Books, 1974)

TREE-LINES

robin fulton

with drawings by harley elliott

new rivers press

1974

copyright © 1974 by robin fulton
library of congress catalog card number: 73-89357
isbn 0-912284-57-9 (paper)
      0-912284-58-7 (cloth)
cover photo by hardie truesdale
book design by c. w. truesdale

some of these poems previously appeared in ARIEL, BORESTO
MOUNTAIN AWARDS ANTHOLOGY, MINNESOTA REVIEW, ¿
STATESMAN, POETRY REVIEW, SCOTSMAN, SCOTTISH INT]
NATIONAL REVIEW, SCOTTISH POETRY SIX, SECOND AEO
SPIRIT, STAND, THE TIMES LITERARY SUPPLEMENT, and
BBC Radios 3 & 4.

This book has been published with the generous support of
THE SCOTTISH ARTS COUNCIL

NEW RIVERS PRESS books are distributed by
                          Serendipity Books
                          1790 Shattuck Avenue
                          Berkeley, California
                          94709

this book was manufactured in the united states of america for
newrrivers press, p.o.box 578, cathedral station, new york, n.y.
10025 in a first edition of 700 copies of which 500 have been
bound in paper, 200 in cloth of which 15 copies have been sig
and numbered by the author.

TREE-LINES

ONE

TWO

THREE

FOUR

FIVE

SIX

ONE

OCH MORLICH

on a spit of sand, a pine on tiptoe, enough
space under the roots for a man to walk through:
they're like a rusted grab abandoned by workmen
decades ago, somehow the tree's still alive

in a wide clearing, a floor of roots to walk over,
no growth in the triangles of dry sand:
the ravel can never be unpicked, the loops all
uneven like a child's first attempt at weaving

in a fertile corner, with earth and junipers,
a giant pine on its side, almost as white as quartz:
it should be in a museum with metal rods
supporting its bones and learned estimates of its age

in the shallows, a stump (surely older still)
with two moulded roots sticking up like horns:
something has been retreating or advancing so
long and stubbornly only the gesture remains

: : : : : : : : : :

FOUR POEMS FROM ASSYNT

1. By Lock Fewin

nothing to be heard, it's like listening for a note
too low or high for the human ear
but knowing it's there and the water is so
still it looks solid and transparent

nothing to be seen moving but for a cloud-
shadow crossing the rock face of Suilven:
it moves like pure spirit made visible and vanishes
and once more the water is opaque and in motion

2. Coming South From Loch Lurgain

morning: Stac Polly is a total wreck, more
total than the puny wreck of a metropolis,
near the rock a human voice breaks open
like toy thunder, the silence snaps shut on it

evening: from the right distance we can see
the Summer Isles levitate above the water
and Cul Beag bright and transparent as a lace
curtain, if we were closer it would ripple in our breath

3.   The Red Pool, River Kirkcaig

nothing could be less colored than this clear water,
I stare through it, my mind clouded with images
of clear water, boyhood is only six inches
under, I can neither reach it nor see through it

on the way home I look south to Ben Coigach
whose top is clear for once: the other side of it
drops right down to a fifty fathom hole
off Geodha Mor, scarcely a mile from the shore

4.   The Names

The hills wear their Gaelic names like old-fashioned hats.   Is Meall
     Dubh no more than a Black Lump?   What will happen to a
     language when it survives only in the names of hills, like the
     ancient pines in ones and twos, the remains of enveloping forests?

A white boat slides between Isle Martin and Aird Point: the casual
     English voices echo across the water almost as loud as the calling
     of migrating geese.   By the roadside a telephone-pole whitened
     by many winters has been singing all day.

In an inlet on the north shore of Loch Assynt we saw a half-sunk
     rowing boat.   Its lines were still visible and it looked as if it
     might be still good enough to retrieve — though perhaps it had
     already settled too far into the life of moss and reeds.

: : : : : : : : : : :

A NORTHERN HABITAT

— Summer is now diminished, is less by him.
Something that it could say cannot be spoken —
As though the language of a subtle folk
Had lost a word that had no synonym.

Norman MacCaig, in 'A Voice of Summer,'
a poem about a corncrake

1.

imagine a lost language, imagine a shadow
per se, uncast, independent:
behind us, seeping into our wet footprints
before us, the empty vaults of a dark wood

a soft weight that lulls the bracken, corrodes
the ancient skin of the loch and heals it again

eyes watching us, whether to attack
or defend, discreet plumage, a scarlet flower,
a green rust on damp hills, a white
antidote to autumnal acids

a shadow not ruled, but ruling its object
a ripple in a stream round an invisible stone

2

awakenings: the ship slopes away
and the drowning voices that will never drown fade

the illusions flicker; yet another replay
of Dresden pulsing like a film of cells dividing

childhood anxieties: is there no
line where day ends and night begins?
the cliff-face of cloud above the pines
always hesitates and dissolves

3

part of my mind is crossed by twisting highland roads:
over the wilderness of lost generations
(only cotton-grass and flanders poppy flourishing)
it has become a habit not to tempt enemies
or providence with straight Roman access

Debussy: a total stranger in those parts but welcome,
he too belonged to a time before clearances
names and ranks chipped with immaculate serifs

I am not the first to have imagined forests returning

4

the ghosts sweat, stumble over birch-stumps
exhale midges: in the scoured glens there is no room
for all of them and many are again dispossessed

the emigrants have returned and I am tongueless among foreigners

5

arriving again I see the moor
like drab tweed: its gaudy life
survives, three inches high

'a second Milky Way in our own'
he said and I measure the tree
in my mind against the original:
the match is perfect yet they repel
each other as stubbornly
as magnets like pole to like

I rediscover skylines
and cause as little interruption
as twenty thirty years ago:
heather springs back behind me
yet my feelings twist like strata
in the bedrock above intrusions

6

rain glitters between the fir-trees
I hold out my hand, it remains dry

the air is photo-sensitive, alive
with the tracks of rare migrating particles

I stand there thinking, an anachronism
lacking even the refined senses of an owl

I move on, leaving my thoughts in the air
behind me, a brief confusion of midges

7

november in the woods:
I sweat in the wind, rasp
off resinous slabs
stack them up for winter

I turn back: my house
is a retreating mirage
and I shall never get near
enough to say: 'I am home'

the wind has gone, my breath
inaudible, each
falling flake a maze
of miniature white crosses

8

the one fir in the garden, stranger
among sycamores, prospers:
a contemporary of mine, now
quite beyond human proportion

a spire above the arthritic branches
where at the end of autumn we gather
cold green apples and think
of summer, its blunt raspberries

9

a sense of security:
each winter the drifts
return to the same place

in the city winter dusk
snow survives on ledges
sills parapets:
a blackboard diagram
abandoned after only
the horizontals were drawn

each nightmare is
open, suffused, sunlit:
the loneliness of the south

10

awakenings: caught like a boulder wedged
for ever between the claws of dried roots

seductive blue shadows on packed snow
a jungle behind suddenly clenched eyelids

in the fault between two dimensions: im-
probable rodcells and conecells

11

elsewhere:
a blood confusion, pangs to deliver a dead child

elsewhere:
the unconceived throng, outlines of shadow

a drugged birth:
the faces of the truly ill belong to a different species

here, behind
glass: neither my father nor myself

here, behind
glass: will none of the names fit? he scowls

: : : : : : : : : : :

TWO

1

what happens to the intolerable space?
we stand here at an unmeasured depth
with wine glasses, overshadowed by flowers
I imagine the surface of the night sky

'the history of broken things' he says smiling
and I remember the beautiful crystal spheres
that somehow survived the minds dreaming them:
the reflections, the curved fragments survived also

'coming home again' she says 'I watch
the lonely waves unfold in the city streets'
I touch a flower, it tears my hand like coral
our words merge as blood whines in our ears

La Cathédrale engloutie next door,
from our own lit windows dance music
and sudden laughter like glass breaking, we grope
across the lawn like shadows on the ocean floor

2

what happens to the intolerable weight?
as if flesh became spirit yet was still
flesh, we stand in a giant glass bubble
on the ocean floor, our ears stop whining

instead 'Mahogany Hall Blues' you cry
I say 'Louisss — you blew that note
five years before I was born'
forty years on and glowing still

(survived like a china cup in an air-raid)
what happens to the intolerable time?
here it is too deep to flow, it weighs
on the incredibly thin glass of our dream

rapture of the deep: those outside
stare in with distorting faces
we can see straight through the drained eyes
of those who are for ever on the point of dissolving

3

the history of sunk things, the divers roll
weightless in clear water before descending,
out of the sun's reach they will remember
a sphere of intolerable brightness

deep enough down in our own element
our element is too much for us, our hearts
race, the music we imagine slows down
as we count survival out by the second

bright coral grows on the broken ships
the all-clear has wailed for a generation
but down here our ears stop whining
as we yield to the intolerable weight

nitrogen narcosis of the spirit:
the rainbow shoals, the transparencies
swirl for ever before the eye-sockets
through which the darkness on the other side stares

5.7.71

24

1

home again, the green
trees sigh in the dawn
their green shadows open
as I walk through them
the night train still
rattling within me
through shadows closing
before closing behind

across the sea always
open glassy between
opaque yesterday
opaque today
curtains I didn't know
were there open, I look
at a square bronze plaque
(dont 40 entants)

the curtains are in-
visible and close
again at once, is all
history like this —
a transparent shadow
closing behind closing
before? I walk home
through green shadows

that open for me spaces
narrower with every step

a day without shadows
a multistorey view
the walls all glass:
I see you cross the square
part of my past that walks
right away from my future

I wave, an absolute
goodbye, my hand throws
no shadow on the wall
waving from the present
no past or future
to disturb with *au revoir*

why don't you look?
isn't my exposure
total? or are the walls
mirrors, that you hide
your eyes and stumble for
the nearest patch of darkness?

as you disappear in it
I am once more opaque

while the spaces
are still open I see:
both of us transparent
make our way between
the blocks of dark that shine
that the light knows not

while the spaces
are still open I see:
the heavy bronze letters,
the doorstep that didn't
flinch, the thin curtain
of my imagination

while the spaces
are still open I see:
green shadows closing,
if I wave you see me
in the disturbance
between future and past

while the spaces
are still open I see:
a man with trowel and brush
crumbling our black shadows
to get at the beauty
of our disjointed bones

june 1971

RAIN

'There are no sliced divisions. Indian music is like water'
(T.K. Jayaram Iyer)

1

there is no *tal,* all is broken
and where all is broken all
is endless

we keep hearing the lost music
behind streaming windows, beyond
the trees where the rain has the voice
of rivers

there is no *rag* either
so without *tal,* without *rag*
the music must be truly lost
and we lost also   two
ghosts with dissolving memories

'the silence beyond silence' you say
still half believing, but I
hear each succeeding silence
echo

the wet veils open for us
will never close

2

it streams down the clear surfaces
it's the imagination that blurs

we forget how to talk, listening
to trees, windows

there is no command yet we obey

standing more and more still
until our whole existence is
a small dry silence in the rain

'the silence within silence' you whisper
not a beginning but a dead end

3

the rain has stopped

we look through the air clearly
without hearing anything
as if it were thick glass

there are no words yet to ask
where is the music the rain hid?
the music on the point of being lost
night after night of rain?
when the words come we will not need them

in the great silence of Becoming
he will meet us familiarly:
his fingers on the sitar-string
will no longer remind us of rain

SURVIVAL

1

birth of an antiparticle in an ocean
of particles: micro-instant death!
our minds are at ease flickering
in the afterglow of remote disasters

2

we are less at ease watching salmon
attempt the impossible: for all their beauty
and muscle-power slashed down in mid-
arch by the waterfall, they have no discretion

3

we admire an early star in the glassy air,
we drive home carefully: a sudden
O.I cc of clear liquid
of insect life quivering on the windscreen

august 1971

passing the Somme, gentle green curtains,
the whole countryside is gentle to those
who travel through it with heavy eyelids
mesmerised by shadows racing the train

until the train stops – and waits and waits
and no-one leans out and asks why

for in the silence where even the grass-hoppers
among the embankment flowers have been stilled
we stare with pale diaphanous faces
at the green light slowly rising like a river

until the train, submerged, is insubstantial
and we drift free – have we been here before?

the green veils part readily,
our footprints leave no mark
in the white fields where so many ended,
in the cramped quarters where most of us began

august 1971

BEGINNINGS

1

the welcome of oil and bandages, while the musicians wait
and the voice: neither bread nor beer I offer but peace of mind

they found his ancestor still crouched in his womb of dry sand

2

in the concrete underpasses and fly-overs the echoing vaults
completed last year but already as old as the virgin desert
a man walking or running is an affront to superhuman dimensions
and his voice like a butterfly wing in the raging of dinosaurs

yet even here music is not impossible: some have heard
at certain corners 'alpha' from stressed metal, 'omega' from walls

3

after the drugged birth, coming home in the sharp dawn
I passed a blackbird singing in a suburban hedge

those three seconds are longer than my allotted span

may 1972

THREE

EPTEMBER THE FIRST

1

e house creaks with a fresh season, I think how old
e noises are and shiver as the lower depths of sleep
ill and expunge memory after memory

ily a few of which survive the dizzying ascent
 the bright surface of morning — 'september the first' we announce,
it something more than a new autumn wind is roused:

stand at the window, green sprigs clutter the street
in flashes, furious and horizontal in the sunlight
at whitens and hurts like a prolonged magnesium flare

shines through me, I am a transparent ghost
i ice skeleton with an unwanted view of the pure
ark horizon as yet hidden by the turmoil of leaves

e leaves that are still green, still putting up
eir annual hopeless resistance, and my shadow
hind me on the warm carpet is still black and faithful

the trees are statues, each leaf curled
for a stone eternity, clawed and hard
as the fronds in a gothic cathedral
                                                 — it seems dark
until I turn the last corner homewards
(past midnight, they'll be sleeping now)
and a giant moon meets me full in the eye
baleful, over-exposed
                                    — like a mind
numbed by a clear view of particulars
too many and too clear a view
and as if longing for an autumn haze
to blur, to comfort
                            — and as I turn homewards
I see: every window in every apartment
walled in, every door blocked,
one continuous wall in the moonlight

no question of any form of life
ever   having existed behind this cliff
whose surface bears the minute stains of centuries
of centuries survived
                                — I shut my eyes
all the particulars merge, a smudged rainbow
remains of my over-exposed view
and my shadow vanishes through my door before me

september 1971

for Ella and Östen Sjöstrand

1

the mists are not quite down on the shorn field

the ghosts are not yet rustling with old age
but stand around me calmly, apple-trees
sun-flowers, all stooped and ripening still

autumn has never haunted me with such wealth
as now: isn't it time to believe the ghosts at last
my feelings simple as maple leaves with crimson veins
my thoughts a generous confusion?

the mists are not quite down on the shorn field
where a reaping-machine waits, beyond harvest,
a long neck a jawbone too rigid to droop

2

in the silence
in the white light:
yellowing oaks
the lake still blue and free
no line of vision blocked

neither flaw nor darkness in the crystal wall

my knowledge is:
acid in the soil
the weight of fruit pulling to its own decay

in the silence
in the white light:
a branch of cherries

my knowledge is too clear
I look straight through as if it weren't there

3

not a ghost but a clear warning:
survival, as the white of a birch bole survives
the rust of autumn

the mind is a silver landscape – one breath
will mist over a lifetime's knowledge:
in the landscape beyond the clear windows
– wastage of seed

the lanes between the red wooden houses
lead me through both landscapes
my breath white in the air

and I too am now one of the ghosts:
we know the warnings, we know – they survive
generation upon generation

september 1971

THE LAST BOAT OF THE SEASON

                          for Lotta and Gunnar Harding

                              1

somewhere outside, sky and sea
are one indistinguishable black

motto for the day has been: *will visitors
please leave, the boat is ready to sail*

town after town, horizon after horizon
on every platform and quay the waving people
have shrunk and vanished most quickly of all

we must be stars in an expanding galaxy
pulled further and further apart from one another

the vodka in my glass sways gently, a small
but clear measure of what's happening beneath

I drink it up
                the empty glass tells nothing

                              2

the night train echoes in the pinewoods
at every crossing the warning bell clangs

my dreams too show a doppler effect
distorting faces and words as they approach
as they leave: total clarity only
for a microsecond

tomorrow, waiting, the last boat of the season

tonight, the train's already past your horizon
known about but unseen like an atom

we can trust our eyes only at arm's length

I look at my watch every five minutes:
a green luminous smudge in the dark, the earth
seen by an astronaut having a bad night

I take it off
          and smother it under my pillow

3

the ghosts say 'we are eternal'
          and depart
Mahogany Hall Stomp plays them out

the richly dying trees are dying invisibly
my own thoughts tinge in the acid soil:
I'm in the dark between two landscapes

the days and the music can always be played again
fresh candles lit in the red holders

we know about the departure of eternal things

what's left?
          your hand on my watch to hide the time

september 1971

1

my friend, old russet ghost
once again at my side?

my senses are like a boat
resting on an autumn lake

thin membranes of air
of water, of eye, of mind

how much to hold
in abeyance — we say

the water is not glass
the air is not crystal

yet our knowledge is held
on a membrane of light

and we no longer fear it:
russet ghost, welcome

the huge white bodies
that drift past by night
with blue tickets pinned
to their unbleeding shoulders

hate against hate:
I try not to feel

I remember yesterday
I was a skeleton
the voices howling through
and no softness left

the day begins gently
like the first smooth inches
of a long train journey:
the distant reunions
inevitable partings
the white deserts, I know

I open my eyes, the black
gives way to blue
I open the curtain, the blue
gives way to white
another barrier broken
a veil torn, I've come
through and stand here
opaque and vulnerable

my russet ghost, old friend

russet no longer, the wind
has cleared space for itself between
your thin branches, I count your leaves
I stare through you at the future

the past throngs out of focus
ceaseless as the reflections
of water on the underside of foliage:
so many summers to forget

your kin, my other ghosts
the ochre, the golden, the mauve
take their turn, leaf
minus leaf minus —

through the curtains of autumn rain
the future throngs out of focus
too much on the point of happening
and I must say: one at a time

my russet ghost, you've gone
welcome my ghost of sticks
you'll creak and creak and survive
but you'll not win my envy
until once more
you are green and vulnerable

october 1971

OPEN AND CLOSED SPACES

for Tomas Tranströme

1

under the rafters like ribs picked clean
a locked door stands with open daylight
on each side and seven generations
of wallpaper looped like old bandages

a long-necked construction crane lumbering
yet precise nudges a jutting beam
and a whole floor cascades right on target
in front of the wide mouths of bulldozers

the machines keep clearing their throats in the dust

2

'only to the next ridge, we'll see *something*'
we count our steps, one hundred two hundred three hundred
we see: another ridge, a grouse cackles
into thin air and back out of it again

and a stag scenting us goes high-stepping
round an invisible corner and vanishes:
our car is a glittering speck in the valley, we pretend
we've reached somewhere and go back getting smaller and smaller

and as we shrink the moor goes on expanding

at home I read letters from foreign friends
I remember their houses, the lakes and forests I've passed,
to save space everything's kept in folders,
music too, wound in black coils

life goes on growing, I learn to keep it
in smaller and smaller spaces, ready to open
at a touch and be large again: outside
daylight always seems endless, at night

I listen to the darkness fumbling at the letter-box

april 1972

FOUR

1

they are riding along the straight roads of their minds
cognisant, never at a real loss for words

they still have faith: 'the stars above' says one
and another 'the final irreducible rock'

the earth's still flat, the holes in space
still covered over like elephant-traps

2

it's windy — a crow tumbles buckles lurches
undignified off-spiral zigzag

on a chimney a granny with a hundred eyes
spins off rags of smoke-signals

in gusts it's like a delirious radar-screen
an act of perception finally gone berserk

DOUBLE VISION

out in the early morning stillness I notice
an ash tree whose leaves are almost open,
a pale static fountain, like a child's drawing
of a roman candle done in pencil because
no-one would lend him the bright colors he wanted

I'm blasted awake by a jet-liner whose noise
is slower than light but penetrates deeper,
it's full of electrical and nervous systems (all
agog) and as it homes on a radio wave
earth must be getter clearer and clearer

I come into my stairway: light from the high roof
divides each flight down the middle,
as I climb up my right eye is blind
my left counts steps for my left foot
while my right foot takes incredible chances

may 1972

ЇERONYMUS BOSCH AND OTHERS
(the forest that hears and the field that sees)

painting a white wall white my eyes ache
along the invisible line between old and new

the white air grows green as evening darkens
across grass and leaves invisibly growing greener

the shadow following my hand has lost its clear edges
among shadows that the flat wall sheds on itself

no-one's painting will hang on that wall I think
sensing the eyes the ears the white intelligence

appraising mine: shapes not of my own devising
swell and threaten as the delicate outlines

wander, coverage, and at my shoulder a tree
sighs, a weary official who has seen it all before

april 1972

NO ANSWER

'my words echo thus in your mind'
I hear his voice echo in my house
in another room, perhaps someone
who was listening has been called away
leaving the record turning turning

the voice is monotonous, dead men
soliloquize and no-one answers

outside nothing echoes, the light
is grey from low thunderclouds
green from sedate full foliage
and a white hawthorn is in blossom
so white it must be furious

may 1972

HE CLOCK

early morning, we stumble out of dreams
cursing the birds whose early morning shift
has been at it for hours, it's like waking in a factory

I go through to my son who's still asleep
despite it all
I'm about to shake him awake when I remember

seeing an abandoned clock with no hands
in a disused railway station where once
a train I was on stopped, no-one knew why, and moved on again

may 1972

REMEMBERING TRAINS

London, midnight, the north train, ready to go,
the last doors locked, but still waiting, is hushed:
the travellers, exhausted, are all prostrate on their bunks,
they are mummies or astronauts prepared for a long journey

Cologne, 2 am, someone half wakens and points
'cathedral' at a brick wall, I take his word for it:
a loudspeaker is soliloquizing at great length
marshalling rows of consonants in deep formation:
no-one seems to get off or on, a station guard
watches, thrumming his polished holster, he understands
but isn't listening, the speech must be for someone else

somewhere else: mile after mile of abandoned track
running alongside our own bright mainline,
at times out of sight under hooding weeds

FROM CERTAIN ANGLES

from certain angles a plane coming in to land
looks stationary: I'll return days
later perhaps and it's still there, a fixture

I remember my grandfather round whom
two generations circled in order:
my own children are circling wider and wider

I think of this on my way to the post-office
a bundle of airmail letters in my hand:
in a few hours they'll be thousands of miles apart

constant seepage, though from here we see nothing:
the steep catchment, its ice-age bones showing,
must be alive with water, an inch down, in the marrow

a breeze, a throng of thistle-seeds like commuters:
some in a many-legged panic along the road
some calm and direct in a high air-corridor
a few at ease going straight to the top on a thermal
on the way up passing others plummetting down

one o'clock, time for the news: the announcer's voice
occupies the entire air-space of the valley
a dense invisible mist of information,
the water far out is black, we hear nothing,
the radio is lying in the sun like a heavy closed book

FIVE

THE SONGS OF ARCHAEOPTERYX

1

en the closed eye discovers it can no longer open
en the foot pauses and knows it will never reach the stone
en the leaves stretch for air and there is no air left
en the seeds fall on rocks that slowly absorb them
en the fish sink straight and the birds fall like boulders
en the closed eye dreams that the world is still working
en the door you locked years ago is still open
en your friends decline invitations you never sent
en the short word you pronounce goes on and on for ever
en the word is so long you can never find the beginning
en your enemies accept invitations you never sent
en the door you have walked through for years is suddenly locked
en the open eye hopes what it sees is a dream
en the birds and fish are frozen tight in their elements
en the rocks fall on seeds that are not seeds but rocks
en the air chokes the leaves and strangles the toughest stems
en the stone pauses and knows it is about to crush the foot
en the open eye discovers it can no longer close

why must it always
be such gentle unfolding
revealing the stones
the sky opening
and the trees all
exposing each other?
you're wearing a yellow shadow
and I can't see your face

why must it always
be full flower
hiding the stones
the sky never closed
and the trees all
hiding each other?
you're wearing a green shadow
and I can't see your face

why must it always
be such hesitant folding
revealing the stones
the sky closing
and the trees all
exposing each other?
you're wearing a red shadow
and I can't see your face

why must it always
be full snow
hiding the stones
the sky never open
and the trees all
hiding each other?
you're wearing a white shadow
and I can't see your face

do you like me in yellow? yes
wear it when you're twenty
and your eyes are white

do you like me in green? yes
wear it when you're forty
and your eyes are red

do you like me in red? yes
wear it when you're sixty
and your eyes are green

do you like me in white? yes
wear it when you're eighty
and your eyes are yellow

knock knock who's there? don't
answer, he's wearing
an old brown shirt and he burns everything

the rain pricks and the dew stings
the dew stings and the wind bruises
the wind bruises and the sun melts
the sun melts more than it should
the sun melts and the snow annuls
the snow annuls and the frost reminds
the frost reminds and the rainbow promises
the rainbow promises more than it should
the rainbow promises and the cloud reveals
the cloud reveals and the air chokes
the air chokes and the ice preserves
the ice preserves more than it should

the rain is a needle the dew is poison
the dew is poison the wind is a fist
the wind is a fist the sun is a tiny
secret we have unlocked at last
the sun is a secret the snow is a drug
the snow is a drug the frost is a scalpel
the frost is a scalpel the rainbow is a sour
disease we give each other at last
the rainbow is a disease the cloud is a mirror
the cloud is a mirror the air is dead tissue
the air is dead tissue the ice is a huge
eye that will watch over us to the last

do you like me in ivory? yes
be ivory when you're twenty
sun fades on the dull wood

do you like me in jade? yes
be jade when you're forty
sun fades on the dull steel

do you like me in steel? yes
be steel when you're sixty
sun fades on the dull jade

do you like me in wood? yes
be wood when you're eighty
sun fades on the bright ivory

knock knock who's there? don't
answer, she's flesh
and blood and shivering in the rain

why must it always
be such a cold beginning
revealing the stones?
you want to be remembered
in ivory —
if only you would wear
a yellow shadow I
could see your face

why must it always
be perfect blossoms
hiding the stones?
you want to be remembered
in jade —
if only you would wear
a green shadow I
could see your face

why must it always
be such a cold ending
revealing the stones?
you want to be remembered
in steel —
if only you would wear
a red shadow I
could see your face

why must it always
be perfect crystals
hiding the stones?
you want to be remembered
in wood —
if only you would wear
a white shadow I
could see your face

although the silence deafens the tireless uproar of the voices
although the air exhausts the lifespan of the wings
although the sun edges every colour with black
although the rain softens the wiry ancient roots
although the frost persuades innocent flowers to open
although the silence cracks under you like ice
although the smooth stones outstare the quick eyes
although you remember only what catches your feet and hands
although the echoes distort the pitch of the plucked strings
although the strings are stretched for echoes they can't give
although your hands and feet suffer from lack of memory
although the eyes waste themselves on the smooth stones
although the ice cracks under you in stealth and silence
although the innocent flowers open and meet their reward
although the roots dry and split despite the rain
although the colors always darken to original black
although the wings crumple beneath the weight of the air
although the voices batter themselves against the silence

TWO

1

I
am watched day and night by the river's eye
that cannot close

I
am listened to by the rock faces that answer
in my own words

I
am touched by the hand of winter soothing away
all feeling

my name
is a blue shadow that flickers on a white wall

2

you
are watched day and night by leaves clustered
in ambush

you
are listened to by the stones you crunch over
in your flight

you
are touched by the green hand of summer
staining your skin

your name
is a brown shadow that soaks into the earth

3

he
closes his eyes, all his tormentors
are still watching

he
refuses to speak, all the cliffs answer
in his own words

he
turns his back, the rain still seeps
through and through

his name
is a grey shadow hovering on a grey wall

4

she
sleeps, hoping the spring rain will wash
her knowledge away

she
talks and talks, hoping to forestall
the next question

she
smiles at the camera, hoping for
a blurred picture

her name
is a white pebble sinking in black water

5

it
lies dormant cowering for centuries
in the veins of leaves

it
writhes caught like a thin coil of smoke
torn by the wind

it
flares in agony at the flashlight
and vanishes again

it
has no name and is easily forgotten

6

we
are many, a single eye in the darkness
watches us all

we
have many voices, the echo from the rock
never varies

we
touch each other with our many hands
winter spreads

our names
merge, an impenetrable shadow

7

they
count the eyes in the night sky and crouch
under trees

they
listen to the voices of the leaves predicting
hunger and thirst

they
are outnumbered by the spring rain
their hands rust

their names
all sound the same to you to me

8

everyone
keeps turning away from the red eye
that never closes

everyone
has a voice he never recognises
as his own

everyone
reaches into the frosty air with fingers
that curl like leaves

everyone
has a name no-one else remembers

has no-one
turned his red eye on the secrets crawling
in the green night?

has no-one
forced silence on the sheer cliff, ice
on the muttering water?

has no-one
survived the poisonous rain with his hands dry
his mind like glass?

has no-one
left his shadow growing like a black crystal?

1

the dark wood is all around me
here in the broad day

the people sitting on the grass
are green, transparent

the shadows are green also but loom
between me and the sun

my own shadow is part of the wood
it rustles under my feet

I do not hesitate, knowing
the straight paths curve

spore hovering in the air
wavers at my breath

if I were to speak to myself here
my words would be soft snow

treacherously white and warm
I remain silent

the white sun is all around me
here in the dark wood

the wood offers no protection
against darkness against flames

layer after layer   opening:
the aroma of dead seasons
the air we breathe is thick with spore

the layer we start from   below:
trees preserved between pages
the leaves rise in a haze of dust

the earth steps taper   down:
a torch an eye close to the wall
thin red lines in the rock

always counting back   subtracting:
our forest ancestors turn
we slip between their thin shadows

absolute history   the beginning:
rock-bottom, your mind glints
like mica, your shadow begins to climb

mirror on the wall
my voice answers itself
from the dim forest
openings
the cliffs of silence
amplify my steps

mirror on the wall
my leaning shadow
darkens the wet surfaces
of leaves
the blind forest
multiplies my image

mirror on the wall
the blue veils are thin
the trees stitched on them
waver
I see myself
staring through myself

mirror on the wall
the veils are diaphanous
the veils are a dense mist
closing
the eyes are spent
the breath clears from the mirror

4

all the words are
what happens in silence

all the light is
the dark flowing after

all the music is
at the edge of a cold sea

all the stones are
what the eyes hide

between two words
a cliff without echoes

between two shadows
a match struck in the sun

between two waves
the ice groans in spring

between two stones
a third glints like an eye

the rain washes   blackens all the roads
the flower opens   stains the clean earth
your words flutter   cloud the air and die
leaving echoes that multiply in the shadows
your steps survive   the witnesses follow
night heals   your shadow grows white
dawn breaks   ocean and forest darken
(when the hand opens all the eyes close)

all the roads are shining   the rain is black
the earth is swept clean   the seeds are dry
the air is a smooth mirror   your words breathe
but no mist clouds your steady image
the witnesses forget   your steps recede
your shadow is transparent   even by day
earth is whiter and whiter   sky darkens
(when the eye opens all the hands close)

mirror on the wall
my voice gets no answer
from the chill forest
closings
the cliffs of silence
do not hear my steps

mirror on the wall
my leaning shadow
glitters on the melting
ice
the blind forest
soaks up my image

mirror on the wall
the black veils are heavy
the trees stitched on them
are rigid
I hear myself
listening hearing nothing

mirror on the wall
the veils are impenetrable
the veils are a thin mist
opening
the eyes are pristine
the breath clouds the mirror

layer after layer   closing:
the aroma of crushed seasons
the air we breathe is sour and clean

the layer we start from   above:
birds pinned in level flight
the white wings open for ever

the earth steps taper   up:
the horizon shrinks slowly, curves
round the pale green oases

always counting forward   adding:
our children uncurl, weightless
stare past us with crystal eyes

absolute future   the end:
cloud-burst, your mind mists
like glass, your shadow is transparent

the white sun is all around me
here in the dark wood

the people sitting on the grass
are black, incandescent

the shadows are black also but open
between me and the sun

my own shadow is part of the light
it flares under my feet

I hesitate, the straight paths
run straight through me

spore hovering in the air
glows as I breathe

if I were to speak to myself here
my words would be black crystals

treacherously black and cold
I remain silent

the dark wood is all around me
here in the broad day

the day offers no protection
against flames against darkness

OUR

1

eye of wind
blurred with rain
eye of day
closes early
eye of needle
suspicious
eye of cyclone
in a trance
eye of the blind
taking your measure

2

ear of grain
under the heel
ear of night
(the owls have eyes)
ear of winter
lost souls
ear of rock
nothing to declare
ear of the deaf
weighing your words

3

tongue of water
the stone is cold
tongue of air
searching searching
tongue of bell
obedience
tongue of flame
once bitten
tongue of the speechless
shaping 'guilty'

4

finger of rain
chaste clammy
finger of dark
no traces
finger of scorn
folded
finger of earth
(green fingers!)
fingers of the dead
infecting you

5

bones of the risen
applauding you
bones of the fallen
tucked under
bone of contention
smiling
bones of the fallen
blocking your way
bones of the risen
burying you

6

finger of rain
promiscuous
finger of light
leaving stains
finger of scorn
erect
finger of earth
(hands off!)
fingers of the living
luring you

*

tongue of ice
not a word
tongue of air
furred with snow
tongue of bell
false alarm
tongue of flame
twice shy
tongue of the living
'innocent innocent'

ear of grain
opening secret
ear of day
(the owls are blind)
ear of summer
cupped
ear of rock
a ready answer
ear of the living
deaf to your words

eye of wind
all-seeing
eye of night
never closes
eye of needle
accommodating
eye of cyclone
dead calm
eye of the living
looking past you

FIVE

1

the dark is never perfect
your free fall will not
be invisible for ever —
how deep is the dark?
not deep enough

your secret journey will be
common knowledge long
before the end — how
far does the dark reach?
not far enough

your private accumulation
of word upon word
will be sifted for evidence
how inward is the dark?
not inward enough

the dark is never perfect
sooner or later pin-
pricks burn through
— the light touches your eye
you are incandescent, a red
flare in the black sky

when you stood there naked
your thin shadow splayed
on the white earth,
the winter sun staring
straight through you, we
too were staring through you

and had little to fear:
your arthritic joints
creaked in the wind,
your roots a tight knot
holding you down, we knew
you'd keep your distance

while we kept warm
running, our footprints
crisp in the snow,
we were young enough
to outwit the season
to survive in the empty spaces

— suddenly you are here
again, you have sprung
your ambush,
who would have thought
you'd choose *this* season?
you are monstrous and green

crowding in on us:
you have crowded out
the summer sun,
swallowed our quick shadows,
we are rooted, blind
in your thickening shade

can barely hear your triumphant rustling

mirror on the wall
the blue streams divide
and divide in the green mind
the lush plants survive
they strangle each other and
survive

mirror on the wall
the crystals multiply
each bigger than the last
remember your own shape
an inch more an hour less
you'll still be there

mirror on the wall
forest within forest
is the outward journey
endless? it stops when
you reach the small hole
at the centre and disappear

4

colours float in the deep water
blush and fade with each season
trail complementary shadows
retire from each other gracefully:
you enter their world flailing
for a lifeline that isn't there
your free fall accelerates:
why doesn't the water drown
your screams, offer *some* resistance?

shadows float in the deep light
some have roots some have jaws
some eat their young, all
pursue avoid eat each other:
you enter their world crouched
head tucked knees folded
you roll softly almost weightless
your free fall has been arrested:
why don't you choke on the light?

5

mirror on the wall
the red streams divide
and divide in the white mind
the ferns of ice survive
they strangle each other and
survive

mirror on the wall
the crystals multiply
each smaller than the last
remember your own shape
an inch less an hour more
you'll still be there

mirror on the wall
forest within forest
is the inward journey
endless? it stops when
you reach the tall cliff
at the edge and disappear

when you stood there clothed
your green shadow brimmed
on the green earth,
the summer sun staring
somewhere behind you, we
rested in your soft light

and had little to fear:
your ancient arms bore
an easy burden,
your roots a foundation
for our world, we knew
you'd keep us close to you

while we kept cool
always knowing the distance
to the next shade,
we were young enough
to be content with the season
to survive as it survived

— suddenly you are here
again, you have sprung
your ambush,
who would have thought
you'd choose *this* season?
you are monstrous and naked

crowding away from us:
you have exposed us to
the winter sun,
released our frail shadows,
we are running, seeing
for the first time the empty spaces

that echo to your triumphant creaking

the light is never perfect
your free fall will not
be visible for ever −
how deep is the light?
not deep enough

your common journey will be
a lost secret long
before the end − how
far does the light reach?
not far enough

your public monuments
of word upon word
will be decently buried
how inward is the light?
not inward enough

the light is never perfect
sooner or later pin-
pricks burn through
− the dark touches your eye
you are opaque, a black
flare in the red sky

X

1

I
look the river in the eye and smile at
its dusty beginnings

I
tell the rock faces what to say
and they are dumb

I
walk on deep water whose thin ice
bears me

my name
is a blind score on ice-age rock

2

you
can now see far through the trees
you stripped

you
silence all the stones under your feet
as you return

you
inhale the acrid fumes of dead seasons
and thrive

your name
is a tough clawed root that won't budge

3

he
stares through the dark and sees their eyes
shut at last

he
talks at last and the silence is
afraid to reply

he
opens his hand and winter at last
has a warm touch

his name
is a hard green shoot in the wilderness

4

she
awakes, exposed to the cold spring rain
that leaves her dry

she
is silent, knowing that the last question died
in the winter mud

she
smiles, her reflection hard as ice
in the black water

her name
is a crystal of ruthless symmetry

5

it
returns without fail millionfold
in leaves and grass

it
settles on us, soaking through the soft
pores of the air

it
burns out deserts, freezes hard
in the living eye

it
has a name all try to forget

6

we
are many, our single eye outstares
the scowling darkness

we
speak with one voice, the echoes jabber
in their flight

we
touch everything within reach
we are possessed

our names
are clouds bulging above the winter trees

7

they
count the eyes in the night sky then
count their own

they
breathe ice on the leaves to silence their
subversive rustle

they
gleam shoulder to shoulder as the rain
steams off them

their names
leave no space for you for me

8

everyone
says the red eye is a dull stone
the stone stares

everyone
says the voices have all withered and fallen
there's no reply

everyone
reaches out to fill the spaces between
the earth is white

everyone
says his name, the ice-crystals multiply

has no-one
been outnumbered, one to one, in the night
full of eyes?

has no-one
been shouted down by his own words echoed
from the silent cliffs?

has no-one
left a blurred picture, a standing-stone
in the red rain?

has no-one
left a burnt shadow on the white wall?

SEVEN

:::::   1

no flower without earth
no earth without space
no space without flower

flower without earth
ice in the everlasting
mind, a cruel mirror

earth without space
exiled to the spot
in perpetuity

space without flower
silence in the absolute
dark, a perfect sphere

earth without flower
conservation of energy
the stony petals endure

space without earth
the black circles close
in, close in

flower without space
icy blossoming
in the disorders of time

no flower without space
no space without earth
no earth without flower

:::::   2

why all this
rumor? are the words
in leaf at last? it's spring
the gates are all open and the empty road waits

why all this
brooding? are the words
overblown? it's summer
the gates are all shut and the empty road waits

why all this
rustling? are the words
crisp and dead? it's autumn
the gates are all open and the empty road waits

why all this
hush? are the words
forbidden? it's winter
the gates are all shut and the empty road waits

why all this
hesitation? a word
out of season? the gate closed
or open and the empty road still waiting?

no hand
without a flame to start back from
no tongue
without a wall of rock that never answers
no ear
without a wind howling desecrations
no eye
without a sun waiting with a flame to blind

no flame
without a hand learning soon to be wary
no rock
without a voice that can do without answers
no wind
without an ear attuned to temptations
no sun
without an eye that knows when to close

small green window of earth
small blue window of sky
small black window of night

small green window, a cold beginning
small blue window, a short journey
small black window, a cold ending

small green window, pain at the start, tearing up roots
small blue window, free fall, nothing to hide behind
small black window, pain at the finish, clearing the land

small green window, the fields are dense with black flowers
                that open only at night
small blue window, the fields are dense with blue flowers
                that remain invisible
small black window, the fields are dense with green flowers
                that die before they open

small green window, faults in the glass
our eyes are cold, earth is no longer
green, sky blue, night black

small green window of departing
small blue window of distance
small black window of arriving

:::::   5

the hand admits and the tongue denies
the tongue denies and the ear confesses
the ear confesses and the eye conceals
the eye conceals more than it should
the eye conceals and the earth opens
the earth opens and the space closes
the space closes and the flower forgets
the flower forgets more than it should
the flower forgets and the sun chills
the sun chills and the time slips
the time slips and the mirror imagines
the mirror imagines more than it should

the hand is a rock the tongue is ice
the tongue is ice the ear is an echo
the ear is an echo the eye is a tiny
cloud that smothers us at last
the eye is a cloud the earth is a flame
the earth is a flame the space is a breath
the space is a breath the flower is a pale
drop that poisons us at last
the flower is a drop the sun is a wound
the sun is a wound the time is a fault
the time is a fault the mirror is a deep
shadow that swallows us at last

::::: 6

no hand
without a flame it can't withdraw from
no tongue
without a wall of rock that always answers
no ear
without a wind smothering the voices
no eye
without a sun whose flames have needle-points

no flame
without a hand that never learns to be wary
no rock
without a voice begging for false answers
no wind
without an ear convinced of its own guilt
no sun
without an eye that never closes in time

::::: 7

why all this
rumor? are the words
home at last? it's spring
the gates are all broken and all the roads are crowded

why all this
whispering? are the words
in camouflage? it's summer
the gates are all guarded and all the roads are crowded

why all this
hissing? are the words
turncoats? it's autumn
the gates are all broken and all the roads are crowded

why all this
hush? are the words
deaf and dumb? it's winter
the gates are all guarded and all the roads are crowded

why all this
panic? a word
in its true color? the gate broken
or guarded and the road crowded with people waiting?

no flower without sun
no sun without time
no time without flower

flower without sun
shadow in the absolute
dark, a blind mirror

sun without time
prison without walls
in perpetuity

time without flower
silence in the everlasting
mind, a perfect sphere

sun without flower
expenditure of energy
the stony petals melt

time without sun
the black circles open
out, open out

flower without time
icy blossoming
in the disorders of space

no flower without time
no time without sun
no sun without flower

march — may 1971

SIX

IN MEMORIAM ANTONIUS BLOCK
(January — May 1971)

DEATH: And yet you don't want to die?
KNIGHT   (Antonius Block):   Yes I do.
DEATH: What are you waiting for?
KNIGHT: I want knowledge.
DEATH: You want guarantees?

Ingmar Bergman, *The Seventh Seal*

::::: **ONE**

'the open spaces are not always open,
in the gloom under the conifers little grows
and the seasons change only the small currency
of nature   the wind in the needles is always the same
and the dry split cones chewed by squirrels
seem ageless   a place for standing still
perhaps envying the trees their roots and toughness
a place also for endless circular journeys

at the wood's edge the real nature of the wood
is more easily seen   the dim caves
opening perpetually into each other
endless choices leading to endless choices
and above, the dark tufts that hiss in the wind
the swaying tops   the boles have grown straight
to their predetermined height   you hesitate
among them   to admire you need distance

perched like ornaments on dim shelves
owls wait for the bewildering sky to darken
and from the wood's edge you can see the birches
silver and standing at ease before the shadowy
straight ranks   they seem impulsive
in spring too green   in summer-light
each a juggler with a thousand tiny plates
airborne   in autumn rusting ostentatiously

it has taken you thirty three years to reach
an understanding with the black shadow of the pine,
in the middle of life the dark wood darkens
you are free to enter or leave   free to measure
to squander yourself measuring what has no end
it is a difficult freedom   giving your eyes
half a lifetime to get used to the dark
before they can see the gentle devious rays

what of the birches?   they always stand out
childlike against the dark pines
their leaves quiver readily   they are full of light
even on dark days   they never brood
strange it should take half a lifetime
to see this fragile game with light
and almost not despair   having known
innumerable closings into darkness

coming across snow you stop to look
at a solitary pine pink in the winter sun
leaning on its blue shadow   there is no white
at all in this white forgetfulness
your eyes need half a lifetime
to get used to winter light   not to be dazzled
by the glare obliterating familiar shapes
but to acquaint themselves with the devious colors
flowing in the shadows that are never black   in the white
fields that are never white   their course has no ending'

::::: **TWO**

news from a wooded country   to a superhuman eye
no two trees are alike   but his eyes
close readily   he dreams of mass-produced trees
and awakens on a white treeless plain   it is real to him

'once   in a glade I saw the sky for the first time
in years   the white light had blackened in my absence
it burned rings on my mind   I can endure the black
sun only in its pastel reflections beneath the trees

once   in a glade I saw a dead leaning birch
reflected in a pool so still the reflection
was in clearer focus than the tree itself   my mind's eye
is too sharp for comfort as I stumble beneath the trees

once   in a glade I cut my name on bark and added
I am in the middle of life   now years on
no longer able to add   I cut again
I am in the middle of life still beneath the trees'

he is walking alone across a white plain   the trees
crowding him in and making his journey difficult
are real enough to him   the white curtains of snow that pass
and pass are real also   from a distance we watch him carefully

::::: **THREE**

the tree   whose green light you praised all
summer
is now
black and infinitely complex against
burnished
pale skies,
hardening in their own time its branches
are as now devious   snaky   crookt

your imagination has gold borders   you turn
idly page
by page
the giant picture book The Rise and Fall
of the Tree of Life   the bark wrinkles   rust
beautifies
fall
each plate shows humanity's
archetypal pose   listening

your imagination also has black borders
season by season it is never quite untrue
as now
you read
'once a man was sitting under a tree'
and the words are true   you are still sitting there
listening
the voice
now is human neither owl nor
the arthritic creak of wood   now
the voice rustles   an incessant whispering
'these were our orders, our orders!'

there is no anguish in the voice   you can't reply
the black borders are a stain spreading inwards
this picture will soon be a pinpoint

::::: **FOUR**

the eye widens
dark grey becomes light grey
what is there for the eye to see?
an aerial whispers 'they're back' — hell-fire
can be avoided at the correct angle
and now someone is boasting: 'if I could break
clean out of your atmosphere
would you scorch me up at re-entry?'

now all of us wake, the eye is red
trees are red also with blue shadows
is there more now for the eye to see?
an aerial whispers 'apple-bright' — did
the first bite at the first apple surprise,
the inside like packed snow not
spilling red? an ideal that hovers
out of reach and survives its own burning

the eye narrows
red and blue become dark grey
what was there for the eye to see?
an aerial whispers 'pre-industrial,
our feelings'   boasting was finished early
and we have worn ourselves all out
at the heavy wooden devices our fathers used
these are our life though they wear our lives away

the eye closes
we nurse the flame that could up and curl all

::::: **FIVE**

the great emptiness between Merak and Dubhe
belongs neither to Merak nor to Dubhe

we are deceived by day   our eyes shimmer
widen   cloud over with a blue mist

we bask under a giant tree   we point
at flowers within reach along the horizon

we are clairvoyant, hypersensitive:
a pinpoint of light is a distant train
growing smaller and smaller with someone waving
— we forget who it was we parted from

towards nightfall our eyes clear
the blue mist of innocence thins away

the outer darkness opens   eyes glint
now peering through screens of foliage
becoming transparent and invisible

'the outer darkness'   we repeat the phrase and point
then hesitate as ripple after ripple
widens out   the curves fade and break
the ripples widen inwards mercilessly

Merak and Dubhe are pinpoints   they flicker
on a moist light-sensitive membrane

the great emptiness between them is not theirs

::::: **SIX**

how near   laced clouds are torn in blue air
invisible turbulence
branches with no leaves have put out flowers

spring after spring   they fold into each other
the old scents were never old
they still taste new as the first autumn frost

you breathe freely   walk through an airy house
with all the doors wide open
expecting to recognise the faces and the lost voices

year after year   they open out to each other
the black lines round the edges
melt away   but still not everyone is here

not everyone finds the invisible doors open
'I still see them large as life'
they are invisible specks on your glass horizon

how far   the blue air is too clear for comfort
thinking a little darkness will help
you close your eyes   your eyelids have become transparent

::::: **SEVEN**

white   like a magnesium flash
for an early indoor photo   the white
family faces stare in a black mist

gold   false spring sun between
one blizzard and the next hurrying after
heaven is a blue eye   against such
glaring innocence we wear dark glasses
and keep our thoughts to ourselves in their knowing shades

green   a conspiracy to lull
the restless and keep hidden the white flowers
until they are no longer white   and fall

gold again   (the test for gold is
it will survive acid)   this gold
rusts through and through in the bitter air

'those are my seasons'   his eye is clear
breaking the white light into a spectrum
whose colors play on us as we count
losses (losing count)   how many
in the black mist? in the green? in the gold haze?

he closes his eye on us   we are pale again
as he walks masterfully away   becomes
transparent   we do not envy his gifts

what kind of guilt does he have   likened to
trout lazing and watchful near the still surface
sides radiant in the occasional filtered gleam
back dull against waiting buzzard and heron?
his style makes me ask   his style paints the buzzard
on glass   balances the true to scale heron
on a hair-thin stalk that would snap at the first movement

I ask also because he can change his style at will
his guilt a pale green stain spreading in the air
(spring at last!)   his mind a winter palace set
the cut crystal gleaming like ice on the point of melting
the transparent walls streaming with refractions
'I shall retire to it when the stale bandages
are unwound   resurrection has a bad smell'

I ask with less and less style   guilt for what?
he answers with more and more 'think of cloud images
piled and luminous on a becalmed ocean'   I think
of the depths full of killed ragged things being eaten
the predators also need style to clutch at survival
but what I think I keep clear of his style   doubtless
his guilt will survive   it will still be beautiful tomorrow

the same persistent invitation   'my mind
has many mansions'   though in each dream
or bout of waking I have never gone further
than a long stooped attic with a dusty floor
at times in the distance I have heard
a piano echoing   the mansions are civilised
some imitator of Mozart, music
designed to echo from curled pillar-tops
but here in the cloying silence I stare at
rough triangles and incomplete equations
scratched on the dusty floor   they are unchanged
(what *was* Archimedes writing on the sand?)
here's a trapdoor   that's new   is it
a trap for me?   it groans open and wind
howls   vertiginous depth
of clear air   who would have thought
him capable of such perspectives?
dark green for forests light for fields
blue for reservoirs red for roofs
and people small enough to be invisible
more, his imagination has touched reality
(another mark of civilisation)   white
giant flowers with misty petals and red
centres gently waver
precision-planted   blossoming dead on time

I look up   vertiginous also!
the roof is open   high in the clear air
black rings converge   in free fall
too late I see
their predetermined common centre   is me

118

description of a happy era   why does your black
hand write white words on black
paper?   you look up and bare your black
teeth in a smile   the hair you've overdone
it's too white
and the trees also
frosted at midsummer by a sun so
black it's almost bursting into color

are there any survivors?   you point vaguely
to a corner of white shade and as I approach
I see them   they have made themselves transparent
(ultimate adaptation) and maintain life
of a sort cowering
from the black light
those who have been exposed have stained edges
and are nudged constantly away from the purest shade

even there, furthest in from the black day
they contend   'is there no *absolute*
white, *absolute* safety?'   if there is
it's worth fighting for, ghost eat
ghost, their teeth rip
black holes in each other
the torn ones run screaming out in the black
light, become invisible   the victors hunch
closer more murderous   they are still transparent still pure

::::: **ELEVEN**

they have forgotten even their names
a green flood washes their memories
smooth   all day the sweetness of crushed grass

'we are at one with antiquity'
they say, having forgotten everything
they awake each morning convinced
there was no night

they listen to voices in the trees
they yield to temptation

some of them smiling stumble
into pools and vanish

some of them have been preserved
between the pages of old-fashioned books
and old ladies finger and crumble them
smiling

a few   a very few   dried
flakes are in safe-deposits
in marble halls supported by everlasting pillars

::::: **TWELVE**

a dream   the diver watches his own drowned face
at an indeterminate depth, neither green nor blue
almost failing, almost not his face
but after each plunge
the soft splinters waver together again   almost

the dream is lonely   the diver turns his back on us
and we on him
we see each other's faces and know they are not ours
we circle round each other
terrified of getting out of hearing distance

the white walls bounce back our bruised voices
the white walls of our minds
of Europe of our picture of Asia
master the cruel stains, soak
the colored mess of a generation
and are for ever white   our shadows move on them
still with pristine edges
our understanding stops
at the fine but monotonous distinction between
our black shapes
and their white ground
it stops dead
at the idea of the white absorbing even the black

we cringe beneath the echoes

outside in daylight
distorting as thick glass   the drowned faces go on melting

::::: **THIRTEEN**

your world has four glass walls   they seem
to keep their distance but you are never sure

when they keep their greatest distance   the world is safe
and undistorted, each leaf is
in its place and seen to be in its place
so pure the glass   an acrid scent
yet seeps through (something sour
you once forgot)   miniature claws
begin to fondle your nerve-ends   tingling
you pace from wall to wall measuring how
they move further and further apart with your fear:
the remote still-life on the outer surface
of your wet eye
is unmoved
as its invisible roots outflank
and pierce your invisible stronghold

when the walls keep their least distance   the world
may still be safe   a tree raging
upside down on the inner surface
of your calm eye may still be a mime
even though the storm is earnest and water
streams down the sides of your dry world
you bask   your fingers idly count without
counting how with your shrinking fear
your world shrinks:
you watch the trees bulge and shrivel   you are unmoved
your breath mists over the world outside
and the world melting on the glass   until
you have no breath left to spread on the glass

pure verticals   pure horizontals   (marks
of civilisation)   the surfaces are stone-hard
ground polished rigid at beautiful right angles
an example to the incorrigible curves of nature

we listen to the incorrigible voices off-stage
prompting, confusing

ultimate adaptation   to be transparent
to stand against the wall and be one with the wall
an eye without substance yet seeing everything

'somewhere in this elegant city there must be
a soft stone   a secret that will yield to the foot
somewhere in this decaying city the surface must give'

'there *is* no surface'   say
the voices of those whom the surface has long since absorbed

thick veils of mist pass   reveal
obscure reveal obscure the heavy spire
I have stopped praying for them to pass forever
and expose an absolute skyline
even if the air stopped perpetually blue
the hunched stones would still turn their backs
my insistent questions would still flow
smoothly off the round shoulders   vanish
in dim runnels at the depths of the castle walls
the stones would dry quickly in the clear light
and my eyes also exposed would soon darken
everlasting day become night
— flecks of mica   millions of tiny eyes
would keep me under surveillance in the shadows

the space within the thin walls is greater
than the space without   there are long queues
waiting within   they shuffle past slowly
reveal obscure reveal obscure and mumble
what *do* they remember? why do they ask
such pointed questions and accept such
lying answers?   I have stopped praying
for them to reach the front of the line quickly
but I do wish well to those few
who are less vigilant about keeping their places
who strike a match now and then and see
millions of eyes staring in the mist droplets
— those who wish to become pillars of salt
find their wish granted immediately

::::: **SIXTEEN**

his doubts have divided subtly   they spread
in the air all around him pliable and frail

the desert where humankind was a thin cloud
the sheer rock faces   a youthful invention

in the middle of a dark wood that is neither dark
nor light but a dialectic of shadows

hesitations   perpetual green rustling
incessant adaptation to the air

'but beyond the wood the empty spaces
are not inventions   they wait to be discovered

between the light and the dark there are no shadows'
'my roots have not budged   I'm standing on them still'

::::: **SEVENTEEN**

'the forest is my natural element   it has
no walls   there is nothing to separate
one fear from another   I pursue my doubt
as it manoeuvres down endless green corridors

the seasons are confident   boles erect   seed
inevitable   among them I equivocate
I grope in the light   see my way in denser shadows
my unease is my knowledge my confidence'

'the forest was a complex dream you've outgrown
it's a house of many mansions   all around you
doors you never knew about click shut
your time is guaged by the discreet closing of doors

soon there will be only one window   from it
you will look at a white treeless landscape
your breath on the window will be white   it will wrinkle
and freeze   in the hard light its ferns will glitter faintly'

UR POEMS FROM ASSYNT: Assynt is an area of N.W.
  Scotland of spectacular geological interest.
NORTHERN HABITAT:
  part 5 - 'a second Milky Way in our own' -
        Beyond the divisions,
        the broken intervals,
        they move, those
        drawn by the impossible dream
        like a second Milky Way
        in our own.
  (Osten Sjostrand, 'Motbilder,' DROMMEN AR INGEN GASAD
        (Bonniers, 1971))
DERWATER: 5:7:71 - Louis Armstrong's death reported
'rapture of the deep' - a common name for nitrogen
narcosis.
DOWS: 'dont 40 enfants' - a fragment that stuck in my
mind from seeing a plaque in a Paris side-street in memory
of a group (of whom 40 were children) who were taken
away and murdered in a German camp.
N: the quotation is in Peggy Holroyde's INDIAN MUSIC
(Allen & Unwin, 1972).
INNINGS: the first two lines are from inscriptions in an
Egyptian pyramid.
ANSWER: line 1 - Eliot's disembodied voice on a record
of THE FOUR QUARTETS.
MEMORIAM ANTONIUS BLOCK: part 5 - Merak and
Dubhe are the two stars in the constellation of the
Plough which are in line with the Pole Star.
'Observing the stars, we experience an emptiness which is
not theirs' - Miroslav Holub, ALTHOUGH (Cape, 1971).